Myths & Legends

MICHELLE SHALTON • PENNY UNIACKE

Editorial Board
David Booth • Joan Green • Jack Booth

D1309686

STECK-VAUGHN
Harcourt Achieve

www.HarcourtAchieve.com

10801 N. Mopac Expressway
Building # 3
Austin, TX 78759
1.800.531.5015

Ru'bicon © 2006 Rubicon Publishing Inc.
www.rubiconpublishing.com

Project Editors: Miriam Bardswich, Kim Koh
Editorial Assistant: Lori McNeelands
Art/Creative Director: Jennifer Drew-Tremblay
Assistant Art Director: Jen Harvey
Designer: Jeanette Debusschere

6 7 8 9 10   5 4 3 2 1

Myths and Legends
ISBN 1-41902-399-3

CONTENTS

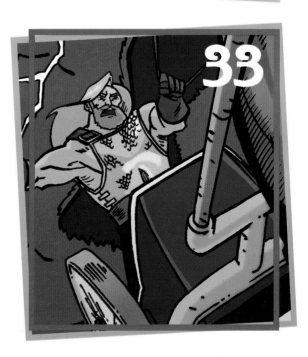

Introduction

The crashing thunderbolt ... the twinkling stars in the sky ... the mosquitoes biting you — ever wondered how they began?

A long time ago, people tried to explain the mysteries of nature and teach moral values through stories. These stories, which have been told and retold over thousands of years, have become the myths and legends that we still read about and tell ...

Flip over the pages and enjoy these tales of long ago, from countries all around the world.

Achilles' Heel
(A Greek Legend)

Illustrations by Mike Rooth

Achilles was a Greek warrior. When he was a baby, his mother held him by one heel and dipped him into a magic river. The magic water made Achilles safe from all harm. Unfortunately, his mother forgot to wet the heel she was holding, so it was not protected by the magic water!

For ten long years, the Greeks and the Trojans fought a bitter war over land and honor. The Greeks wanted to capture the city of Troy. No matter what they did, the Greeks could not reach the walls of the great city. This was because Hector, the Prince of Troy, was a magnificent warrior. No one could beat him in a battle. He killed many great Greek warriors. The war dragged on for many years and thousands of soldiers on both sides were injured or killed.

The Greeks knew that only Achilles could beat Hector. But Achilles refused to go to war. His friend, Patroclus, decided to put on Achilles' armor and fight in his place. Hector thought Patroclus was Achilles and killed him.

warm up

- What Greek myths or legends have you heard of, read about, or seen in a movie? Share one with the class.

- Think of your strengths and weaknesses. Do you let anyone know what they are?

FYI

The Ancient Greeks believed in many gods and goddesses. They always looked to their gods and goddesses for help, especially during wars and times of trouble.

CHECKPOINT

How do you think Achilles would have reacted to his friend's death?

Upon hearing this tragic news, Achilles grew angry and joined the battle to avenge his friend's death. Achilles fought and killed many Trojans. All the time he was looking for Hector.

Hector became frightened after hearing tales about Achilles' strength. He asked Apollo, God of Light and Truth, for help. Apollo helped Hector by covering him in a cloud of mist, so that he could hide from Achilles during battle.

CHECKPOINT

A Trojan was a person from Troy. Today, when we describe a person as a "Trojan," we mean that person is brave and never gives up. Do you think this is a good description?

Once Achilles reached the Kingdom of Troy, he demanded that Hector come out and fight. At first, Achilles could not see Hector through the mist, but soon he spotted the Trojan warrior. Hector ran around trying to escape, but Achilles chased him and struck him dead with his sword.

Now the Trojans were in trouble. Their greatest warrior Hector was dead, and it seemed that no weapon could harm Achilles.

avenge: *to get revenge*

Once more, the god Apollo came to the help of the Trojans. He told Hector's brother, Paris, about Achilles' weak spot, his heel. During the next battle, Paris shot a poisoned arrow at Achilles' heel and ended the life of one of the greatest Greek heroes.

wrap up

1. The term "Achilles' heel" is used to describe someone's weakness. For example, "Her Achilles' heel is her laziness." What do you think your own Achilles' heel is?

2. Using a fact chart, list the details from the legend. In one column write the mythical details, and in the other write the realistic details.

WEB CONNECTIONS

Use the Internet to find more information about the war between Troy and Greece. What caused the war to start? Who were some of the people involved? How did it end? Organize your information in a chart and either print it out for your friends or email it to them.

MOUNT OLYMPUS SCHOOL YEARBOOK

 CLASS OF

⚡ MOST LIKELY TO SUCCEED

ZEUS (Zooss)

Nickname: God of the Sky

Claim to Fame: Ruled the halls of Mount Olympus

Ambition: To be supreme ruler of all things

Biggest Contribution: Saved his brothers and sisters from being eaten by their father

Favorite Memory: How he and his brothers divided the Universe into three sections — the Sky, the Sea, and the Underworld. Each brother ruled a section.

⚡ MOST LIKELY TO HOLD A GRUDGE

HERA (Hair-a)

Nickname: Goddess of Marriage

Claim to Fame: Ability to change into different forms ... especially into a bird

Ambition: To marry Zeus

Biggest Contribution: Had many monuments named after her

Favorite Memory: In a jealous rage, she sent snakes to attack Hercules.

monuments: statues or buildings created to remember someone

Illustrations by Mike Rooth

ANCIENT GREECE

⚡ MOST DISLIKED

HADES (Hay-dees)
Nickname: God of the Underworld
Claim to Fame: Got kicked off Mount Olympus and now rules the Underworld
Ambition: To own all the souls of the dead
Biggest Contribution: Trained a three-headed guard dog
Favorite Memory: Kidnapping Persephone and making her his queen.

⚡ MOST POPULAR MALE

APOLLO (A-poll-o)
Nickname: God of Light and Truth
Claim to Fame: Top student in music class
Ambition: To offer help and advice to friends
Biggest Contribution: Helping Paris defeat Achilles by telling him about Achilles' weak ankle (Achilles' heel)
Favorite Memory: Turning King Midas' ears into those of a donkey.

MOST POPULAR FEMALE

ATHENA (A-theen-a)

Nickname: Goddess of Victory, Wisdom, Courage, and Crafts

Claim to Fame: Born from her father's forehead

Ambition: To have a city named after her

Biggest Contribution: Helping to kill Medusa and using Medusa's head to decorate her shield

Favorite Memory: Taking revenge on Paris for not letting her help Achilles defeat Hector in battle.

CLASS CLOWN

HERMES (Her-mees)

Nickname: Trickster and Messenger God

Claim to Fame: Guided the souls of the dead to the Underworld

Ambition: To have a planet named after him

Biggest Contribution: Loaning his invisible helmet and flying sandals in battles

Favorite Memory: Ending a fight between two snakes and using them as a staff.

BEST LOOKING MALE

ARES (Air-ees)

Nickname: God of War

Claim to Fame: Almost died from being stuffed into a jar by two giants

Ambition: To have a zodiac sign named after him

Biggest Contribution: Defeating enough enemies to cover his throne with their skin

Favorite Memory: The first blood stain on his spear!

BEST LOOKING FEMALE

APHRODITE (Af-ro-die-tee)

Nickname: Goddess of Love and Beauty

Claim to Fame: Causes people to fall hopelessly in love with one another

Ambition: To be a matchmaker

Biggest Contribution: Introducing Paris to Helen thus creating one of the greatest but most tragic battles of all time

Favorite Memory: Marrying her husband Hephaestus but falling in love with Ares.

wrap up

1. Which god or goddess would you like to be? Why? Take a poll of the class to find out which god or goddess was most popular.

2. Draw a picture of your favorite god or goddess. Be sure to include any characteristics you've learned from reading the yearbook.

THE GIANT BEAR

warm up

Have you ever felt hungry before?
How did that make you feel?

CHECKPOINT

Notice that "Mohawk" is spelled the same way for one or many.

A long time ago, there was a Mohawk village along a great river. One day, some Mohawk hunters discovered the tracks of a Giant Bear. They saw the tracks many times in the days to come. Then the animals began to disappear from the forest. The Mohawk knew that the Giant Bear was killing and carrying off the animals.

The people in the village soon became hungry. Their meat racks were empty. One of the chiefs said, "We must kill this Giant Bear who is taking the animals from the forest."

A party of hunters set out in search of the bear. They soon came across his tracks in the snow. They followed the bear tracks for many days. Suddenly, the Giant Bear appeared in front of them! The hunters shot their arrows at the bear. To their surprise, the arrows failed to pierce the bear's thick hide. Instead, broken arrows fell from his tough skin.

The angry bear charged at the hunters as they fled. Only two hunters escaped and returned to the village to tell the sad tale.

Many other parties of hunters set out to destroy the Giant Bear. They all failed.

In the village, there lived three brothers who were great hunters. One night, all three brothers dreamed that they had tracked and killed the Giant Bear together. In the morning, they told each other about their dreams. The oldest brother said,

"We must go after this bear."

The brothers gathered their weapons and went after the Giant Bear. They soon came upon the tracks of the great beast. They followed the trail, keeping their arrows ready. For many moons they followed the tracks of the bear across the Earth. The tracks led them to the end of the world. Suddenly, the brothers saw the Giant Bear leap from the Earth into the sky. The three hunters followed right behind — they jumped together into the sky!

After many moons, the animals of the forest returned. The meat racks were full again. The people were grateful that the Giant Bear had gone and they wondered what had happened to the hunters. One night, the people looked up into the night sky at the Big Dipper. They said, "Look! There are the three brothers chasing the Giant Bear!"

wrap up

1. Imagine that you are a news reporter. Write a report about what happened when the three hunters set out to kill the Giant Bear.

2. Create a wanted poster for the Giant Bear. Describe the bear and tell why you're hunting it down.

WEB CONNECTIONS

Using the Internet, find out more information about the Big Dipper. Draw a picture of the Big Dipper and write three new facts that you have learned about it.

Ananse the Spider

AN AFRICAN LEGEND

warm up

Have you ever had to prove yourself by doing a series of tests or challenges? How did you do?

CHECKPOINT
What do you think it means to "spin stories"?

A long time ago in Africa there lived a spider named Ananse. He was known for spinning beautiful spider webs wherever he went. As much as Ananse loved spinning webs, he loved to spin stories as well. But all the stories belonged to the Sky God, so Ananse was not allowed to tell them. He wanted to tell stories so badly that he decided to ask the Sky God for permission.

16

One day, Ananse spun a silk web up to the sky and bowed before the great Sky God.

"O, God of All Things," he said. "I want to spin great stories for my village. What is the cost of telling them?"

The Sky God looked at Ananse and laughed, "Someone so small could never pay the price!"

"I may be small, but I am clever and will pay whatever price you ask," insisted the spider.

The Sky God looked at Ananse and said, "My stories are too valuable to put a price on them. You may complete four tasks instead. Bring me the following creatures: a python, buzzing hornets, a leopard, and a fairy."

"These are difficult tasks for anyone, let alone a tiny spider, but I will bring you these four creatures," Ananse promised.

Task 1

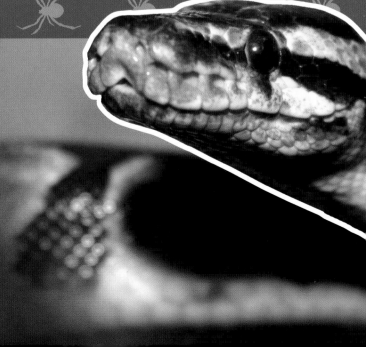

Ananse the Spider headed for the river to complete his first task. As he walked along, the spider pretended to have an argument with someone about whether or not a branch was longer than the great python. The python overheard Ananse arguing with himself. He told the spider to measure him to prove that he was indeed longer than the branch. Ananse told the python to lie down beside the branch. Once he did that, Ananse took the vine and quickly tied him up.

Task 2

The spider continued on to the forest and brought with him a bowl to complete his second task. Once he heard the buzzing of hornets, he climbed a nearby tree and sprinkled water on them and himself. He then told the hornets that it had begun to rain, so they had better take shelter in his bowl. They thanked him for his kindness, only to be captured by the clever little spider!

Task 3

Ananse the Spider then set off in search of the leopard's tracks so he could complete his third task. Ananse dug a hole where he spotted the tracks and covered it with leaves. When he returned the next day, he heard the cries of the leopard at the bottom of the pit. The leopard begged the spider for help, and he finally agreed. Ananse took two bamboo sticks and stuck them on each side of the wall. He told the leopard to place his paws on the sticks to climb out. The leopard did as Ananse told him, but little did he know that a cage was lying at the top of the pit. Once the leopard reached the top, Ananse quickly closed the door of the cage.

Task 4

For his final task, Ananse created a wooden doll and placed mashed yams in her hand. Then he covered the doll with sticky fluid from a gum tree. Once he was done, he placed the doll under a tree where he knew fairies liked to play. No sooner had Ananse placed the doll than he saw a fairy gracefully flying around in search of the yummy yams. Once she began eating them, she discovered that she was stuck to the wooden doll! Ananse the Spider was thrilled. He had completed all the tasks Sky God had given him!

Ananse the Spider spun a big web around the python, the hornets, the leopard, and the fairy, and then threw a thread up to the sky to bring them to the Sky God. "O, God of All Great Things, I have completed all four of your tasks. Here are the python, the hornets, the leopard, and the fairy. Now may I have your stories so I can tell them to my village?"

The Sky God was quite surprised that a tiny spider had completed such difficult tasks. "Greater and mightier people have come before you, Ananse, asking for my stories and I have given them the same tasks but they failed. Your request is granted. From now on, my stories are yours and shall be known as spider stories."

Ananse graciously thanked the Sky God and happily spun his way back to his village to tell his first story. As time went on, Ananse the Spider traveled from town to town, spinning more and more of his spider tales.

wrap up

1. Use a character trait organizer to describe Ananse. Be sure to provide examples from the story.

2. Create your own series of tasks that you would give Ananse to complete.

WEB CONNECTIONS

Go to your school library or use the Internet to find more stories about Ananse the Spider. Read one of the stories you found to a friend.

WHY THE EARTH SHAKES

Earthquake Legends From Around the World

warm up

- With a partner, brainstorm all of the things you know about earthquakes. What questions about earthquakes would you like answered?

- What do you think it would feel like to be in a house during an earthquake?

Earthquakes can be described as the shaking or rolling of the Earth's surface. They happen along "fault lines" in the Earth's crust. Earthquakes can be felt over large areas, although they usually last less than one minute. Over the years, people have tried to explain why earthquakes take place. Here are some legends from different parts of the world.

1 ASSAM

There is a group of people living inside the Earth. Sometimes they shake the ground to find out if anyone is still living on the top. When children on Earth feel a quake, they should shout "Alive! Alive!" so the people inside the Earth will know they are there and stop shaking the ground.

2 SIBERIA

The Earth rests on a sled driven by a god named Tuli. The dogs that pull the sled have fleas. When they stop to scratch, the Earth shakes.

3 WEST AFRICA

The Earth is a flat disk, held up on one side by a huge mountain and on the other by a giant. The giant's wife holds up the sky. The Earth trembles when the giant stops to hug his wife.

4 NEW ZEALAND

Mother Earth has a child in her womb, the young god Ru. When he stretches and kicks as babies do, he causes earthquakes.

5 CENTRAL AMERICA

The Earth is square. It is held up at its four corners by four gods. When the gods decide the Earth is overcrowded, they tip it to get rid of the extra people.

6 ROMANIA

The world rests on the divine pillars of faith, hope, and charity. When the wicked deeds of human beings make one of the pillars weak, the Earth shakes.

divine: *sacred or holy*

FYI

The Richter scale is used to measure the force of an earthquake. Earthquakes below 4.0 on the Richter scale usually do not cause damage. When an earthquake reaches 7.0, it could cause a lot of damage. Many people could be hurt or even killed.

wrap up

1. Draw a picture of your favorite earthquake legend. Explain why you chose this legend.

2. Create your own legend about earthquakes. You might wish to draw a picture to go with it.

WEB CONNECTIONS

Do you know what you should do in case of an earthquake? Go online and find out what safety steps you can take during an earthquake. Write a list of five safety tips that could be printed in your school newsletter.

THE LEGEND OF ELDORADO

On a map, find South America. Once you've found it, look for Colombia. What other countries and bodies of water surround Colombia?

A LAND OF GOLD!

Gold at the Bottom of the Lake!

Imagine if you read these headlines in the newspapers. Would you go rushing to find some of this gold? Well, many people did, when word got around about this incredible land of gold in South America.

Legend has it that thousands of years ago, a king appeared on the top of a mountain overlooking Lake Guatavita in Colombia. His body was covered in gold dust. The king floated to the middle of the lake on a raft and dropped gold into the very deep lake as an offering to the gods.

This story has spread far and wide. People from all around the world have traveled to South America in search of the treasure. The lake has even been drained several times. Thousands have died in the quest. But no one has found this mystical gold.

MYTHS AND LEGENDS

Legends are usually based on facts about a real person or events. However, because the story has been told and retold over and over again, the details in the story might change, so it becomes a mixture of fact and fiction.

Myths are usually about the supernatural world, with gods and goddesses as the heroes and heroines, and monsters and evil creatures as the villains.

MYTHS AND LEGENDS OFTEN INCLUDE:

1. A hero or heroine who shows qualities such as courage, loyalty, honesty, and patience.

2. An evil villain out to destroy the hero or heroine or to harm the world.

3. Conflict between good and evil.

4. Good always wins over evil.

5. A message that tells the reader how to behave.

ELDORADO

Gaily bedight,
A gallant knight,
In sunshine and in shadow
Had journeyed long,
Singing a song,
In search of Eldorado.

But he grew old —
This knight so bold —
And o'er his heart a shadow
Fell as he found
No spot of ground
That looked like Eldorado.

And, as his strength
Failed him at length,
He met a pilgrim shadow —
"Shadow," said he,
"Where can it be —
This land of Eldorado?"

"Over the Mountains
Of the Moon,
Down the Valley of the Shadow,
Ride, boldly ride,"
The shade replied —
"If you seek for Eldorado!"

— *By Edgar Allan Poe*

bedight: *an Old English word meaning "dressed"*
pilgrim: *a person who travels to a holy place*

CHECKPOINT

The word o'er means over.
The apostrophe replaces the letter "v."

wrap up

1. Retell the story of the knight and his search for Eldorado.

2. With a partner, write your own legend about someone who travels to Eldorado in search of the gold. Include the elements of a legend (see page 22). Share your legend with the class.

THE FOUR DRAGONS

(A Chinese Tale)

warm up

Brainstorm the different things that you know about dragons. Have you read a story or seen a movie with dragons in it? What did the dragons look like?

Long, long ago, there were no rivers or lakes on Earth. There was only the Eastern Sea, in which lived four dragons: Long Dragon, Yellow Dragon, Black Dragon, and Pearl Dragon.

One day, the four dragons flew from the sea into the sky. They soared and dived, playing hide-and-seek in the clouds. Suddenly, Pearl Dragon stopped and shouted, "Look! Down there!" He pointed down to Earth.

Many people had laid out fruits and cakes, and they were burning incense sticks.

"What's the matter?" asked the other three dragons.

CHECK-POINT

What are incense sticks? Have you seen or smelled them before?

Illustrations by Mike Rooth

"Listen," said Pearl Dragon, "I think they're praying."

A woman was kneeling on the ground. A thin boy was strapped on her back. She raised her incense sticks.

"God of Heaven, please send rain quickly," she said as she looked up to the sky. "We need to give our children rice to eat."

"There has been no rain for a long time," said Long Dragon. "The crops are withered, and the fields have cracked under the scorching sun."

"Oh, these poor people!" said Yellow Dragon. "They will surely die if it doesn't rain soon."

Black Dragon nodded. "Let's go and beg the Jade Emperor for rain," he said.

---

withered: *dried and shrunk*

25

He leapt into the clouds. The others followed close behind. They flew toward the Heavenly Palace.

The Jade Emperor was very powerful. He was in charge of all the affairs in Heaven, on Earth, and in the sea. He was not pleased to see the dragons rushing in.

"What are you doing here?" he asked. "You should be staying in the sea and behaving yourselves!"

Long Dragon stepped forward and said, "Your Majesty, your crops on Earth are withering and dying. I beg you to send rain quickly!"

The Jade Emperor was listening to the songs of the fairies. He was upset at being bothered. "All right," he replied. "Return to the sea right now. I'll send some rain tomorrow."

"Thank you, Your Majesty!" The four dragons bowed and went back to the sea.

Ten days passed and not a drop of rain came down.

The cries of hungry children filled the

air. The starving people began eating bark, grass roots, and even white clay.

The four dragons felt very sorry for the people. They knew the Jade Emperor only cared about pleasure and did not care about the suffering people.

"We must do something to help these people," said Long Dragon.

"What can we do?" asked Yellow Dragon.

CHECKPOINT

What do you think the dragons might do to help the people on Earth?

Gazing at the vast sea, the Long Dragon suddenly said, "I have an idea!"

"What is your idea?" the other three demanded.

"Look, is there not plenty of water in the sea where we live?" asked Long Dragon. "We could scoop up the water and spray it toward the sky. The water will fall like raindrops and save the people and their crops."

"What a brilliant idea!" exclaimed the other three dragons.

"But," said Long Dragon thoughtfully, "the Jade Emperor will not be happy if he learns of this."

"I will do anything to save the people," Yellow Dragon said firmly.

"Let's begin," said Black Dragon.

"We will never regret it," said Pearl Dragon.

exclaimed: *cried out*

The four dragons dived into the sea and scooped up water in their mouths. Then they flew high into the sky and sprayed the water all over the parched land. The four dragons flew back and forth all day. The sky grew dark all around. Before long, the seawater became rain pouring down from the sky. The people cried and hugged one another with joy.

"It's raining! It's raining!" sang the happy children.

"The crops will be saved!" the happy farmers cheered.

---

parched: *dry*

On the ground the wheat stalks raised their heads and the rice stalks straightened up.

The God of the Sea noticed these events and reported to the Jade Emperor.

CHECK-POINT

What do you think the Jade Emperor would do?

The Jade Emperor was furious. "How dare the four dragons bring rain without my permission!" he shouted.

He ordered the Heavenly Generals and their troops to arrest the four dragons. They were brought back to the Heavenly Palace.

"Get four mountains and place them upon these dragons so that they can never escape!" the Jade Emperor ordered the Mountain God.

The Mountain God used his magic power to make four mountains. He pressed them down upon the four dragons. They were trapped under the heavy mountains.

The four dragons did not regret their actions. Instead, they decided to carry on helping the people. They turned themselves into four rivers, which flowed past high mountains and deep valleys, crossing the land from the west to the east and finally emptying into the sea.

And thus were formed China's four great rivers — the Heilongjiang (Black Dragon River) in the far north, the Huang He (Yellow River) in central China, the Changjiang (Yangtze, or Long River) farther south, and the Zhujiang (Pearl River) in the very far south.

FYI

Chinese dragons are a symbol of power, greatness, energy, and good fortune. Unlike Western dragons, they are worshipped, not feared and hated.

wrap up

1. In a small group, role-play one of the most important events in the story.

2. Write a newspaper article about how the four dragons helped the starving people on Earth.

WEB CONNECTIONS

Using the Internet, choose one of the great rivers of China and gather more information about it. Use a chart to organize your information.

The dragon boat race is one of the oldest Chinese traditions. There are many different legends about the dragon boat race. The most common legend is about a poet named Chu Yuan who lived about 2,000 years ago in the Kingdom of Ch'u. Chu Yuan was a faithful and honest servant of the emperor. The people of Ch'u loved and respected him.

Sadly, the officials of the Kingdom of Ch'u were evil and dishonest. They were jealous of Chu Yuan. The officials falsely accused him of being disloyal to the Emperor. As a result, he was banished from the kingdom.

Chu Yuan was heartbroken. On the fifth day of the fifth month

GON BOAT RACE

(in the Chinese calendar), he threw himself into the Mi Lo River.

The people of Ch'u were devastated. They rowed out in their boats beating loudly on their drums. They were trying to scare the fish and water dragons away from Chu Yuan's body.

Today, the dragon boat races act out these frantic attempts by the fishermen to protect Chu Yuan.

The Ch'u people also threw rice dumplings into the river so Chu Yuan would never go hungry. These special dumplings were wrapped in bamboo leaves so that the fish would not be able to eat them. Today, these rice dumplings are still eaten on the fifth day of the fifth month, in memory of Chu Yuan.

CHECKPOINT

What did the people do when they learned their hero was dead?

FYI

Today, charities hold dragon boat races to raise funds.

Teams compete in long boats decorated like dragons, with fearsome heads, scaly bodies, and long tails. When the races begin, the rowers move their boats forward to the beat of drums. The winning team is the one that first grabs the flag at the end of the race.

devastated: *overcome with grief*
frantic: *desperate*

wrap up

1. Using a storyboard, recreate the different events that happened in this legend.

2. Write a notice about Chu Yuan's death for a local newspaper.

WEB CONNECTIONS

Using the Internet, find more information about the tradition of dragon boat racing. Make a poster about an upcoming dragon boat race. Include date, time, and place.

THE CHALLENGE OF THOR

By Henry Wadsworth Longfellow

I AM the God Thor,
I am the War God,
I am the Thunderer!
Here in my Northland,
My fastness and fortress,
Reign I forever!

Here amid icebergs
Rule I the nations;
This is my hammer,
Miölner the mighty;
Giants and sorcerers
Cannot withstand it!

These are the gauntlets
Wherewith I wield it,
And hurl it afar off;
This is my girdle;
Whenever I brace it,
Strength is redoubled!

Jove is my brother;
Mine eyes are the lightning;
The wheels of my chariot
Roll in the thunder,
The blows of my hammer
Ring in the earthquake!

Force rules the world still,
Has ruled it, shall rule it;
Meekness is weakness,
Strength is triumphant,
Over the whole earth
Still is it Thor's-Day!

FYI

Norse legends came from ancient Scandinavia in northern Europe. They describe a mythical world of gods and goddesses, giants and demons, trolls, dwarfs, and elves.

Norse gods and goddesses lived in a mythical place called Asgard, high up in the clouds. Their mission was to fight evil.

gauntlets: *gloves*
girdle: *belt*

wrap up

1. Draw a picture of Thor. Include details from the poem. Give your picture a title with an adjective describing Thor, e.g., "Mighty Thor."

2. Read the last stanza with a friend. Explain what Thor means by those words.

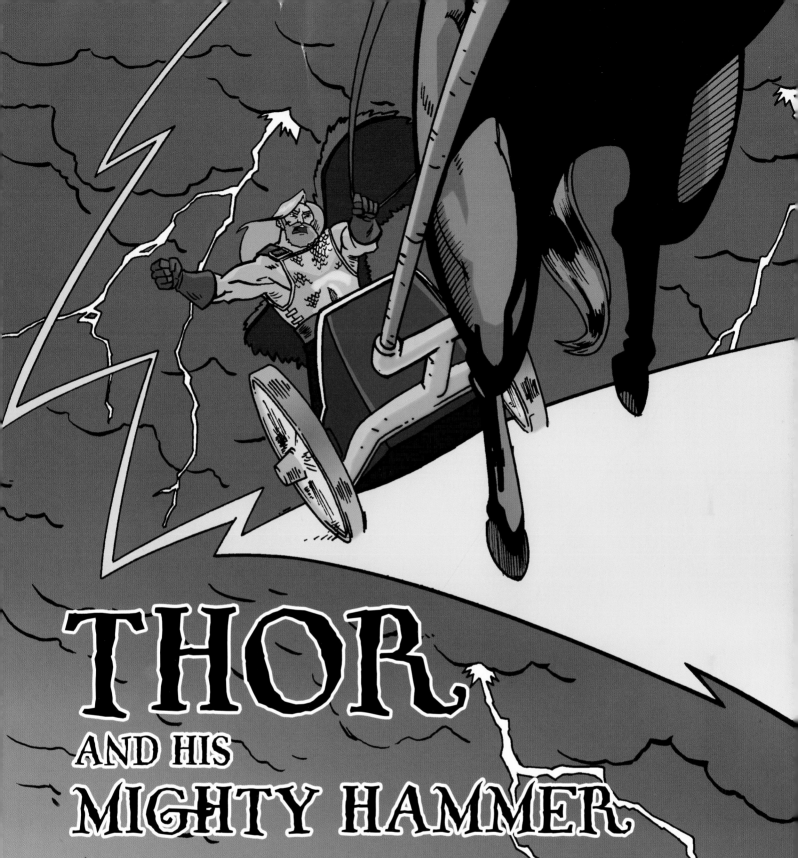

THOR
AND HIS
MIGHTY HAMMER

AN ANCIENT NORSE LEGEND

The skies shook with thunder as Thor charged across in his chariot. He was desperately searching for his hammer.

warm up

Discuss different items you own that mean a lot to you. How would you feel if you lost one of these items?

33

Loki, God of Mischief, stopped Thor and asked: "Did you misplace your hammer, Thor? Is that why you charge through the skies causing thunder?"

Thor roared back, "I would never misplace my hammer! No, the evil giants must have stolen it! Since you're so eager to help, you must go down there and get it back!"

Loki found the king of the giants tending to his horses. "Did you take Thor's hammer?" he asked the king.

The giant king replied, "Yes, I took Thor's precious hammer because he is weak without it. If he is weak, I have a better chance of defeating the gods. I will only return the hammer if Thor brings me Freya, Goddess of Love, for my wife."

Loki reported the giant king's demand to Thor. Together, they went to ask the goddess Freya if she would marry the giant king. She angrily refused.

CHECKPOINT
Predict what Thor will do.

Thor did not know what to do. He asked the other gods and goddesses for advice. They suggested that Thor dress up as a bride and trick the giant into believing that he was Freya.

"Never!" roared Thor. But he really wanted his hammer back.

Finally, seeing no other way to get his hammer back, he agreed to the plan.

Dressed as a bride, Thor rode to the land of giants. Thinking that Thor was Freya, the giant king invited "her" to a great feast to celebrate their marriage.

Thor was hungry. He ate and ate and ate. The giant king watched in amazement. "How is it you are so hungry?" he asked his bride-to-be.

CHECKPOINT
Notice how Thor explains why he is so hungry.

Thor replied, "I was so anxious to see you that I did not eat for eight whole days!"

Touched, the giant king lifted Freya's veil to give her a kiss. He jumped back at the frightful fiery glow of "her" eyes.

"Do not be afraid, oh King," said the false Freya. "My eyes are red because I have not slept in eight full days awaiting my visit to your land."

The giant was relieved and asked his sister to bring him Thor's mighty hammer. He placed it in the lap of his bride as a symbol of their promise to marry. Thor's heart leapt with joy at the sight of his hammer. He grabbed the hammer and struck down the giant with it. Thor returned home and continued to chase and destroy the evil giants.

wrap up

1. Imagine you are Thor. Write a short journal entry describing how you tricked the giant into returning your hammer.

2. Brainstorm some superheroes that share Thor's characteristics.

warm up

Tasks are jobs that you have to complete. What tasks do you complete every day?

CHECKPOINT

Read the text under the pictures first, and then proceed to read the bubbles.

FYI

Heracles, also known as Hercules, was the greatest hero in Greek mythology.

THE TWELVE TASKS OF HERACLES

Heracles was a tough little baby.

Everyone loved him but Hera, Zeus's wife, who sent two snakes to kill him.

But Heracles strangled both of them.

For a while, Hera ignored Heracles.

As he grew up, Heracles became stronger and stronger and stronger.

He married and had many children.

Hera hated him for being so happy.

So one night she put a spell on him. Heracles lashed out with his sword, killing imaginary enemies.

When he woke from the spell, he saw that he had killed his own children.

36

Heartbroken, Heracles went to the temple to seek forgiveness.

The priestess said he could make amends by serving his old enemy, King Eurystheus.

The king was frightened of Heracles, so he hid in a pot whenever he came near.

And because he hated Heracles, he gave him twelve deadly tasks.

First, Heracles had to kill the lion of Nemea whose hide was so thick that no sword could penetrate it.

Next, he had to kill the many-headed Hydra, whose very breath could kill man or beast.

Third, he had to capture the sacred, golden-horned deer, an animal as swift as the wind.

The fourth task was to catch a savage boar whose tusks could pierce any armor.

Next, Heracles had to clean out the vast and filthy stables of King Augeas in a single night.

Then he had to to destroy a flock of man-eating birds that hid in a dangerous swamp.

The seventh task was to capture the fire-breathing, marauding bull of Crete.

Next, he had to steal Diomedes's horses, which fed on human flesh.

Then Heracles had to fetch the golden girdle worn by the queen of the Amazon warrior women.

The tenth task was to seize the monster Geryon's cattle, guarded by his two-headed dog.

The eleventh, to collect three golden apples protected by a ferocious dragon.

Heracles's twelfth and last task was the most dangerous of all: to fetch the three-headed guard dog, Cerberus, from Hell itself.

His twelve tasks completed, Heracles returned to King Eurystheus.

The king was dismayed to see him alive, and quickly sent him packing.

Then, to avoid angering the gods, Heracles sent Cerberus back to Hades.

At the temple, Heracles was finally pardoned.

He was content at last, and stronger than ever!

And Hera never bothered Heracles again.

wrap up

1. Make a list of the words that you didn't understand in this story. Find out the meaning for each word and add it to your word list.

2. With a partner, act out one of Heracles' tasks.

3. Create a "Strongest Man" poster about Heracles. Include reasons why Heracles is the strongest man.

FYI

There are over 100 films and TV shows about Hercules, including *The Three Stooges Meet Hercules* (1962), *Chinese Hercules* (1973), and *Popeye Meets Hercules* (1948).

Arnold Schwarzenegger's very first acting role was in the 1969 film *Hercules in New York*.

When the Ancient Greeks wanted to swear, they would say, "By Heracles!"

THE BLACK PEARL OF BAHRAIN BAY

Retold by Suzanne Muir

warm up

Discuss a time when you did something that you really didn't want to do. How did you feel afterward?

A long time ago, Queen Anouba the Caliph's wife went to the royal jeweler to show him a wonderful black pearl.

Caliph: *an Arabic term for ruler*

41

"Can you sell me another of these black pearls?" she asked the jeweler.

"My Queen," said the jeweler. "You can ask me for emeralds as big as eggs, topaz that gleam like a tiger's eyes, or rubies that give off flames at night — and I can place these treasures at your feet. But the stars will fall like rain on your palace before I can find another pearl like this. There are not two alike in the whole world. I am sorry."

A diver named Amry was standing beside the jeweler, quietly listening. Queen Anouba looked at Amry and said, "I will give you 20,000 gold coins if you dive deep into the ocean and bring me another black pearl."

CHECKPOINT

Do you think Amry will do what the queen asks?

At first, Amry laughed. Then he became very serious. "Good Queen," he said, "you are asking me if I want to die. The last diver who brought a black pearl back from Bahrain Bay still turns pale and shivers with fear when his boat passes over the reef."

"Why? What did he see?" asked the Queen.

"My Queen," said Amry, "the coral reef is enchanted.

CHECKPOINT

What do you think "enchanted" means? Think of three other words the author could have used instead.

"When the diver went down into the chasm, the reef began to sting him. He continued to collect shells and suddenly a strange seaweed began to close in around him. It grabbed him around the chest and began to squeeze him. A giant spider crab floated past his face. The crab's eyes glared at him with green rays of light. When his friends pulled him up, the diver was half dead."

"Excellent!" said the Queen. "Since you know where the reef is, you must dive and kill the monster that guards the black pearl. Bring me what I want!"

"Queen Anouba, I have an elderly mother and I am married to a woman whom I love and must protect. I cannot risk my life for a pearl," cried Amry.

Queen Anouba replied, "Come to my palace in the morning." And then she left.

chasm: *a deep hole or opening*

The next morning, Amry dressed in his finest clothes and went to the Caliph's palace. A servant led him to the Queen's living quarters.

When Anouba saw Amry, she dismissed the servants. Then she turned to Amry, her bracelets jingled as she lifted the veil that covered her face. Amry gasped and shielded his eyes from the brilliant light. You see, the Queen didn't have eyes. Instead, there were two black diamonds set in her face, which was as pale as the moon. As he looked into those eyes, Amry fell in love with the Queen.

"I will dive for the pearl at the bottom of Bahrain Bay," he murmured in a trance. "I will leave my blood and skin on the pointed coral, as I have left my heart here."

CHECKPOINT

Do you think Amry will get the black pearl for the Queen?

Early the next day, Amry took his small boat to the reef and began his dive. At the bottom of the sea he noticed an extremely large shell.

"That must be the black pearl," he thought to himself. He swam quickly toward it.

Just as he grabbed hold of the shell, a monster crab rushed up and tried to choke him. Amry fought the crab with all his strength. After a long struggle, he freed his right hand and stabbed the crab with a knife — right between the eyes.

Exhausted and bleeding, he rose to the boat. He climbed on board and fainted. His friends dragged his body to the palace and laid him at the Queen's feet.

Amry finally woke up. He knelt before the Queen and stretched out his hand. Inside was the black pearl.

"Queen Anouba, I have brought the black pearl to you as you requested," he whispered.

Eagerly, the Queen took the pearl. "It is exquisite!" she said. "Tell me what you want, Amry. My fortune is yours."

Amry bowed at her feet and said sadly, "Keep your riches, my Queen. I wouldn't know what to do with them. I am but a diver. By risking my life for this pearl, I have betrayed my wife and my mother, whom I have to care for. You have taken my heart and my soul — I can never hope to have the love of a Queen."

And with those words, Amry died of a broken heart.

Queen Anouba gave Amry's wife and mother his rightful fortune. They promised that Amry's story of "The Black Pearl of Bahrain Bay" would live forever.

> **CHECK-POINT**
>
> Notice Amry's answer.

exquisite: *extremely beautiful*

wrap up

1. Working with a partner, write captions for the pictures in this story.

2. In a small group, brainstorm a list of adjectives to describe the Queen or Amry.

3. Rewrite the ending of this story so that it's a happy one.

WEB CONNECTIONS

Using the Internet, find information about Bahrain Bay. Write a report on your findings.

The Legend of
SLEEPY HOLLOW

By Linda A. Copp

warm up

- Look at the illustration for this poem. How does it make you feel? What do you think the poem will be about?

- Read this poem with a partner and help each other understand the legend.

The *Legend of Sleepy Hollow* is set in a small American settlement around the year 1787. It tells the story of a Hessian trooper who was hit in the head by a cannonball during the American Revolution. According to the legend, the trooper still wanders around Sleepy Hollow searching for a new head.

Have you been to Sleepy Hollow
that tavern by the woods
Where long ago one yesterday
men gathered there and stood,
And told their scary stories
of a Headless Horseman who
Gathered up their countrymen
like potatoes in a stew?

Well, I've been to Sleepy Hollow
and without benefit of glass.
I've listened to the stories
and seen them come to pass.
And hid among the shrubs there
yes, cringed behind a tree.
While that Headless armor gleaming
came whipping up past me —
Wielding out a giant sword,
a massive steel and blade
And riding on an animal
of steel and stone and staid.

I hear him on the bridge, now!
I see the moonlight strike.
His sword and armor riding past
there's nothing that he's like.
A fear, a brute, a cruel thought
I cower in the trees.
I have to sit and ponder him
yet, hope he never sees!

glass: *a drink*

wrap up

1. With a partner, read the poem to the class — be as dramatic as you can.

2. Pick out the words and phrases that tell you the narrator was terrified by what he saw. Using these words and phrases, imagine you are the narrator and send a short email to a friend describing your experience.

ACKNOWLEDGEMENTS

The publisher gratefully acknowledges the following for permission to reprint copyrighted material in this book.

Every reasonable effort has been made to trace the owners of copyrighted material and to make due acknowledgment. Any errors or omissions drawn to our attention will be gladly rectified in future editions.

Linda A. Copp: "Sleepy Hollow," http://www.sunniebunniezz.com/poetry/slehpoem.htm © 2004

Robert Cutting: "The Giant Bear," Permission courtesy of Robert Cutting.

"The Twelve Tasks of Heracles" from Greek Myths For Young Children. Copyright © 1991 Marcia Williams. Reproduced by permission of the publisher Candlewick Press, Inc., Cambridge, MA., on behalf of Walker Books Ltd., London.